EPICS 4:

POEMS #44-#59

BY S. E. MCKENZIE

ii

DEDICATION

To everyone who has been left out in the cold

THIS BOOK IS A BOOK OF SPECULATIVE FICTION.
Characters, companies, governments, places, events, are either
products of the author's imagination or used fictitiously. Any
resemblance to persons (living or dead), companies, governments,
places and/or events, is a coincidence.

CONTENTS

S.E. McKENZIE

CRIPPLED
DEMOCRACY

#44 Crippled Democracy
I

Born free no more;
Laws of Scarcity
Turning many into outlaws

Pushing even more out of the Door;
Feeling unloved and lost
More than ever before.

Miles and Mary held hands
Looked up into the sky
To see which way the wind would blow.

The game they were to play
Was sum-zero;
And nothing more;

No open door
To the Ivory Hall
They were stuck on the bad side of the wall.

Walking by;
Ghetto Queen sits on the steps
Outside of a Smokey private scene;

Reporting those who look suspiciously poor
To Nouveau Gestapo
Not in fashion when shopping at second hand store;

Soon someone Ghetto Queen never knew
Will have their back against the wall;
Could be me could be you;

But it was Mary and Miles;
While Ghetto Queen was buried in smiles;
Accusations fly;

So Ghetto Queen will have it all;

New world order;
Programmed to feel small
For ever more

Living on the bad side of the wall.
So Ghetto Queen can have it all;
On her side of the Public wall.

Integration;
Unknown complication;
Today; ignorance is bliss and cheap;

Dead bodies left in a heap;
Too dangerous
To think too deep.

II

Walls dividing
Haves from Have-nots.
Humans were under the influence

Of assimulated killer bots.

For ignorance was bliss and cheap;
Dead bodies piled in a heap;
Everyone was afraid to think too deep.

Ignorance was bliss;
For it was free;
Higher education was only for the mighty;

Demonization; new religion
For a dehumanized nation;
On the brink of perpetual war

So afraid to ask
"What are we fighting for?"
The walls squeezed in the town called Blue

Micro-managed to be so pure;
Everyone would reach haven;
They were so sure.

III
We hid our minds in the sky

For Love was still hiding there;
Crying and dying; for Love could not belong
In a divided world where caring and sharing

Could not overcome greed and need;
Too many barriers inside a crumbling wall
No access to the Door to the ivory hall.

Complaint driven;
Evidence not needed to be given;
If you own it all.

Ignorance was bliss and cheap;
Dead bodies piled in a heap;
Too afraid of thinking too deep.

EPICS 4

Two worlds;
One that raises the young to be mighty
Another diminishes the young until they crawl.

One side of the wall
Let's you stand tall;
Keep your head down;

If you are on the other side;
Ghetto Queen on a bender
With the watchers who cannot bend;

In the morning her head will hurt so bad
She will feel
It will never mend.

Mega rich guy
Will never have enough
In his world there is no need for love

So inflated; loves to talk tough
Never had to live rough;
His dream was to build a wall

Around every nation; needed no competition

Monopolization
New world order
Chaos for those on the other side of the wall.

Tea is served for charity outside the Door
But won't serve you right
In their store,

Charity for the poor;
Thrown garbage;
Reselling it to the mega poor;

Degradation;
Lost in a dirty used world;
Progressing no more.

False accusations
Lapse in due process
Complaint driven

But no evidence given
Accept screams of pain
While the poorest of the poor

Are kicked down again.
Injury to the mind
Programmed from above

In a world with too little love
And too much hate
Inflating and negating fate.

Bait and switch;
Inflate the opportunity cost;
Youth is lost

Steely face of accusers;
Social abusers;
Sum zero game; no one knows your name;

Winners call us losers.

Miles Tory
Did not plead or beg
Was pressed and crushed like an egg.

Two days of torture
But Miles Tory
Knew his mind; did no plea;

Avoided forfeiture to big brother

Held on the best he could
So that we
From a supposedly gentler time

Would remember
Man's inhumanity to man
Never knowing when the hate began.

But lack of due process
Was not justice
At all;

Ignorance was bliss and cheap;
Dead bodies piled in a heap;
Too afraid to think too deep.

Look down the Ivory hall;
As far as you can;
Can you see a nobler man?

THE END

FIRE

#45 FIRE

I

Chemical change;
Hot Flames
Licking space

Too close to your face;

How did it start?
Some say from a spark;
Others say Fate;

Grew out of control;
Burnt everything in sight;
Fuel fed the Beast with all its might;

Fuel turned a spark into a giant;
Beast enjoyed the feast;
Toxic air everywhere;

Dreams up in smoke;
Fate's joke;
Some said Fate's due was untrue;

EPICS 4

It was up to me and you
To add value;
To everything we do;

To measure the treasure;
A merchant's pleasure
No more;

Fire grew as it devoured fuel;
Fire's rage
Was in control

More powerful than the Queen's rule
Grew as it was fed fuel
Into a Beast no longer just a tool;

Fire was alive but not aware;
Fire could not care
As it spread dread everywhere;

II
Whispered lies
Needing no disguise;
Blocking ears to her silent cries.

Fire was all around
Scorched neighboring ground;
How did Fire start?

By a spark that was never put out;
Our minds were shattered as Fire grew into the Beast
Now we can only shout

"Remember to be true to your dreams

Especially now when shadowed by doubt;
Tearing so many lives apart
Fire did not know how it broke her heart."

III

The peasant king was wearing his crown
While he kept putting us all down;
For he had lost his smile

For he too felt
The burning sting
Of Fire.

King's face was burdened by his frown;
For Fire did not know Divine Rights
Nor Stakeholder Rights;

Fuel was all that Fire knew;
Growing from a spark
That could not die out;

Fire raged and burned down each door
As Fire kept burning it wanted more;
Fuel;

IV

We had No time
For higher learning.
We were left yearning

For those we left behind;
Now only the same
In name;

And nothing more.

We sit on this scorched Earth
Remembering its beauty; its worth
A long time ago, we stand brave

Only in vision
We had to make a decision
We stood at the foot of each new grave

We heard the sound

Of our strained breath;
For no sound came from the ground;
And we dared not to disturb those fallen

Into Infinity's sleep for evermore
Still connected;
We hoped they would be protected

For if they awoke
They would only weep;
Some say they are better off

In Eternal Sleep.
When one;
Unity;

Whole
Infinity;
No beginning or end;

Just a new way to bend
In the circle
Holding so many more

EPICS 4

As flares from the sun
Warmed the snowball
Until it was partly blue

We all speculate
Before we stumble on a fact
Then there is no going back.

It is time to act.

V

One was not the first
Nor the last
Just the one

Without beginning or end
Infinity
Connected everyone

In one way or the other
We would always be
Sisters and brothers

Unity
In a land
That could never be free;

So much was predetermined
Once the spark ignited
Fire would grow to rule.

THE END

STRING

#46 STRING

I

String a long
In this song;
Gravitation

Keeps us down on Earth;
We strum the string
We can't understand everything;

The switch;
The charge;
The Positive; the Negative

In every breath we take
We avoid massive implosion
While we harmonize.

Nature in all its forms;
Defying norms
Just to survive

The ocean comes in waves below;
Particles moving in the sky above; appear slow;
So far away and beyond comprehension;

EPICS 4

As we gaze
We feel love
For the Heavens above;

Massive stars so far way
Flying above our graves in waves.
As Earth rotates away the day.

II
Stability is lost;
When there is no motion;
There is no time;

For the signal to die;
Lost in the vacuum of the black hole
We cry out to Existence

Just for the love of it;
The beat of the Skin Drum
Drives life to come

As far as it can.
And how do we know
How far that can be

We are just mere mortals
And nothing more;
As we live beneath Heaven's Door.

III

Our heart
Can only start
With a spark

So we took a walk
In the park
After dark

Hand in hand
We gazed into the sky
While particles moved

At the speed of light
We could only see this
Cause it was night

We assumed the right
To know the secrets of the Universe
Though we refused to believe

That there was a Multiverse.

IV

We live in this Sphere of Fear
No beginning or end
Light will always bend

For True Life
Must be round
To move

As we lay on this flat ground.

Our hearts
Kept tune
Under the moon

As the Skin Drum
Kept us alive
Our blood circulating

As one;
Infinity;
Connected

To all we can see
And beyond
What some call

Divinity;
Life
Is all we know.

We bend the string

So we can hear it sing
For Harmony
Must be made

Then valued
For evermore
While we live

Under Heaven's door.
Like all the generations before
Our arrival

Our survival
Our revival
We live

For we have so much to give
Before we die;
Never knowing why.

We arrive in this world
Of the breathing
Crying

So afraid of living
And even more afraid of dying
We depend on love for we have nothing more.

THE END

A LEAP IN THE DARK

#47 A Leap In The Dark
I

He closed his eyes
I closed mine too
Together we took a walk in the park;

That was still green;
We gazed into the sky
That was still blue.

We opened our eyes;
There was no space
We just heard slander in our face.

The mob gave us no room to breathe
No room to walk
No room to ride.

The highway crashed through
All we knew
As the watchers

Walked in the middle of the path;
Would give us no room; felt so much doom;
We were belittled by Peasant King's Culture of Obstruction

Kept us pinned
Against the wall;
We felt so small when forced to crawl.

Process to survive was killing us.

Construction of Obstruction;
Life of Destruction
As they built Mega-walls

So high, we could not see

Any of life's Beauty;
We closed our eyes to see
The park and the sky.

Closed eyes can still cry;
We were pinned; left talking to shadows on the wall;
In this cave; there was mandated alienation

Meant to make us feel small;

Stuck in this impoverished Shadow Nation;
They gave us no room
Just to be you and me;

EPICS 4

They told us how to live;
They planned how we would die;
Behind the wall without a door;

Stuck in this Shadow Nation;
So many lost what they had before.
Ghettoized behind the wall without a door.

They see our face
And they blow out smoke
To make us choke;

They have money to burn
As we are still waiting
Our turn.

Ghettoized in segregation;
Monopoly of Cronies;
Broken ties with no integration;

Their land is called Paradise where God we trust
Is written on the ticket to get in;
Have enough tickets then your life will begin.

Otherwise
You will stay stuck in this Shadow Nation
Mandated by alienation; they say

We have no other way to enter Paradise
Until we die; we are left in this Shadow World
Which is as cold as ice.

The only world we are connected to;

Is the Shadow-World;
Where so many chained to walls
Can only see and relate

To shadows in the halls;
When light leaps in the dark
We close our eyes to play in the park.

This world without love
Is as cold as hate; to alienate is their mandate;
While water holds a charge;

The spark felt friction
Took a leap in the dark
Just to feel the energy all around

EPICS 4

Not letting go was your first mistake;
So Rich so Fake;
Peasant King had so much money to burn

As we were still waiting our turn.

Peasant King used his tickets to pay Beauty
To scratch
Every itch.

We see the mob
On the corner; standing there to intimidate;
To alienate is their mandate; the mob falls

For snob appeal.

II

Life was not ours to keep
Once we fall into eternal sleep
In Infinity we may still creep;

Life moves on
Into Eternity
No more winners and losers

Trapped within this food chain
That pins us against the wall;
The Process was killing us so we could survive

Mandated Alienation;
Made us feel so small
When forced to crawl

After shadows in the hall.

III

Rolling Thunder
Light in the sky
Shot at us

And there was no goodbye
As we rolled up
To die;

Peasant King
Had so much money to burn
While we were still waiting our turn

In the dark
We had to leap
To touch the faint light;

The mystery
We were all waiting for
At the end of our war.

Rolled up in sleep
Life inside
Was all that was left for Evermore.

Life leaped into the sky
As we faded away to die
With no time to say goodbye.

Pinned against the wall;
Mandated alienation made us small
Made us crawl.

IV

So many stigmatized
Then rounded up
Behind the wall

Before the fall
We found the hole
Now not too proud to crawl;

We struggled out of the ghetto
While they threw their garbage over the wall
Turning ghettoes into slums;

So they could then sanitize;
Mandated alienation
So lost in this Shadow Nation;

Their subjective manners;
Justified calling us rude;
Pinned against the wall;

Left to feel so small;
Lost in the slums;
The called us bums.

And how they fought each other
To win the right to apply
For government grants

To bury us
After we died
No one was left to care

When the Peasant King lied.

THE END

BROKEN WING

#48 BROKEN WING
I

Hey Eagle
How did you soar
Into the sky

With your wing
So broken and sore?
You lifted me higher

Than I ever felt before.

Militant old man with hair of straw
He didn't have to
Follow the law;

If he had only wings
Instead of hands
He could have flown all over the lands;

In a fashion so migratory;
Creating a peaceful story;
That is not gory; Like Eagle

Fighting to live.
Militant old man with hair of straw
Might learn to love what he just saw.

EPICS 4

Before the big one
Shakes down the earth
Climate change

Deriving fuel
For Hell's fire to burn
While we all know

We will be waiting a long time
For our turn
While space around us is left to burn.

Eagle flew overhead
He flew over those who were dead;
Some were reported missing

And some were not;
The dead were left just there to rot;
Without a care

Watchers weren't there;
For they were watching us;
Creating so much doubt

Hand on the trigger;
Hatred without
Tolerating; shouted out;

And love cried out in pain; needing to give
To live; to feel alive
To survive.

II
Hey Eagle where do eagles fly
When they are not yet
Ready to die.

Hey Eagle
You came back to me
Your wings almost surrounding me;

Even now when nature once free
Is so fenced in
Involuntarily

EPICS 4

By reality so augmented;
Demented;
Future souls so discontented

So many undocumented;
Future's feet so cemented;
Floods and fires

Without known precedent;
Walls that hide the losing side;
Boosts Militant Old Man's pride?

Separation
From the garden
Left fiery footprints

From the other side of Hell.

Hey Eagle, you have so much to tell
You have flown
Above the wall

Our foe so cruel fed the fire's fuel;
Dogma's rule;
Fell here and there;

But you Eagle did not scare;
You fly so high and above it all;
While we are left down here to crawl

In man's economic misery;
Just an extension from ancient history;
Your domain is the sky and in it you fly
And soar

With one wing so broken and sore.

III

With a broken wing
Eagle was pulled
By the other

Force so mysterious
Rewards the curious
With new knowledge; renewed life.

As Eagle flew in the sky sometimes blue
Above the Shadow Nation
That he knew

So demented
Reinvented
Disoriented.

IV
Eagle flew
Into
Destiny

Came back
Stronger than ever before
Learned to fly

With a wing broken and sore.
He flew past threat of extinction
He flew as the symbol of the Nation

What a sensation
For the disempowered
Generation

Hiding in Demented Shadow Nation

As Eagle's son grew
He never knew
How close he was

To never being
Alive
To nest so close to the sky

History cannot change
Future cemented
Into Demented Shadow Nation

Migratory; Eagle flew
Over every border
Below the sky sometimes blue;

Living his very own story

Looking for prey
Quickly fading away
In Demented Shadow Nation

We were tolerated if we didn't speak;
They watch us as we grew weak;
We had nowhere to take a leak.

Eagle recovered better than us;
For us very few who would give us trust;
Soon we would return to dust.

EPICS 4

As Eagle looked on;
So many trees were chopped down
Then gone.

Demented Nation
The young were pushed away
With the future of change

The demented stayed on.
Eagle had birds eye view
Watching humanity lost

Greatest opportunity cost

For Demented Shadow Nation
Walled to separate
Paradise from hell.

Eagle migrated; flying
From season to season
Could see humanity

Without reason; flew past their fate;

V
Still endangered
Eagle soared in the sky
Flew by

The gulls
The skulls
Eagle flew by

Man driving Cadillac
Eagle species was back
Stronger than ever before

Could now pull himself
Off the floor
With a broken wing; still very sore;

Demented; cemented;
Toxic man gets what he can
In this age of rage

Eagle recovered in numbers
Slowly
Flew over the lowly

Made us feel so alone.

Eagle vowed
To never look back;
On the subtle attack

EPICS 4

Of his genome
Black and white
Taking flight

Into the future
Eagle soared;
Mass migration

To flee from his cruel foe;

He flew into tomorrow
And flew by
The man in the Cadillac

Never to look back.

Eagle fought when under attack;
So that he could exist for one more day
Flying away from Demented Shadow Nation;

Eagle would not just survive but thrive.
Beyond mere existence
There was harmony

Power to feel the earth sing;

Eagle soared over the wall
Mass migrator;
He flew where ever he pleased.

For the good of all
Eagle had a birds eye view
And some say he could see it all;

With eyes of the all mighty
In flight;
In fight;

Infinity
Continuity
The power of One

When all things are done.
Eagle
Was having fun.

THE END

The Projector Monster

#49 THE PROJECTOR MONSTER
I

If I could only read your mind
What secrets would I find?
Would I uncover?

Private space for a lover;
Not a fighter any more,
Only after we shut the door;

To discover where the treasure might be;

To see beyond the face
To find the Inner Place
Sometimes so deep

You climb into that sleeve;
And find a new dimension
Of make believe.

New-age corridor of Infinity;
Rage; without form
Or norm;

A place
With space
For those who can see beyond a face.

In a throw away world.

II

She did not say goodbye
For she was not ready to die
Even when she stopped living;

Projector Monster only said good bye
After he lied
Could only be real

When wearing a mask;
Need she ask
How smoke and mirrors;

Swords and daggers
Direct energy;
Select synergy;

Could feed those
Left in this waste land
Under a foreign command

In a land of sand
With very little left to demand;
Even though at one time

There was so much
That was grand.
Completes the task

In a throw away world.

Relativity
New destiny
Free from Bigotry;

New found Equity

Light
Defies
Gravity

In a way, we mere mortals never could;
Just a projection;
Emotion; State of mind.

III
Someone shot
Someone else;
Projector Monster

EPICS 4

Brought up on violent games;
Violent TV shows;
Stares and glares where ever he goes.

The worshipers offer sacrifice to their God
Their enemies' blood
Too proud

To feel lost in a crowd
Where negativity
Justifies barriers to entry;

Speak and you will be accused;
An excuse to abuse
Only way to win

In the Sum Zero Game
They all seek the treasure
And the loser is to blame.

When the treasure cannot be found
For it is still in the ground;
Near the dead soldiers who can't make a sound.

Everywhere
To feel supreme
Barriers

Can make the weak minded scream.

Projector Monster
Just another predator
Condescending

Never bending
Relenting in the dark
While light is freer from Gravity's pull

Than his dark mood;
Feel it brood;
Others so unaware

They have no care
Running with their dog
Pony tails swinging in the air;

Missing all the worlds between here and there.

Nouveau Gestapo
Waves to his Secret Watchers
Of the Shadow State;

EPICS 4

Will never be free in all this Hate.
How they love to discriminate;
Incriminate; Instigate.

Now lost in an ancient dimension;
Forgotten not so long ago;
The same old state of sorrow

Feeds into tomorrow before tomorrow is even there.

Because the treasure cannot be found;
It is still buried in the ground;
Near the soldiers who can't make a sound.

Could never measure quality;
Quantity of Facts
Flooded the gates; before the acts

Of Devastation
Degradation;
Ghettoes hidden in overpriced urbanization.

Pushed many away until they were out of sight;
Soft light in the night; Gravitation
Pulling; reluctant sensation.

Projecting
Onto others so willing
To be stepped on

From above
They never said goodbye
Before the Projector Monster's rage

Made them dead;
Rage projected from his head;
Environmental influence mixed with dread.

IV

Wealthy armies abound;
Remains resting in the ground;
Dead warriors can't make a sound.

Once there was so much might;
Glistening in the light;
Majestic sight pulsating all night;

Now remains
Sinking in sand;
Wealthiest armies in the land

Have lost command.
The ones stuck in the lower realm
Cried out for equality;

In a throw away world;

Wondered what they were fighting for;
The treasure would never be found
For it was buried in the ground

The dead soldiers cannot make a sound
Though they all knew;
No one could ever win this war;

For the walls were in the way;

No freedom from those walls
That caused urban decay
No Freedom from those walls

Which marginalize everyday
No growth; just decay;
Causing stakeholder progress to delay

In a throw away world.

THE END

S.E. McKENZIE

NOISE

#50 NOISE
I

Noise;
Tool for the Old Boys
Before they die; they lie;

While reaching up to the sky
Malice told us not to cry;
Spite told us not to look at him in the eye;

Revenge was always searching for treasure;
For his pleasure.
Hard to measure when always back at zero.

Old Boys are standing under dark clouds;
Young Boys lie in the ground;
Though their presence lingers all around

Space; forgotten face;
No peace in our world;
Rules power in war;

Abounds more than ever before;
Hanging from the sky
A mysterious force holds it all together

Layered dimensions; vibrating;
Can never be owned.
So close to death

Their hearts are turning to stone
They abandon their young; leave them all alone.
Their thirst for power is built on what they own;

Limits what they have to give;
Even though they are dying to live;
Their ability to electrify is gone.

Power;
Creative and destructive;
Negative and positive;

It can marginalize you
Through manufactured lies
That appear to be true;

They marginalize to monopolize
Power;
While they are withering away.

EPICS 4

They hold on to power
With too much might;
Cannot make it right;

While they wait all night
For the morning light
They marginalize to monopolize

While manufacturing powerlessness;

They smile; they trivialize content of character
For at times they have none;
Though if they did, life would have been better for everyone;

They did not know what they had done
While their pollution.
Was blocking out the sun;

No surplus energy to find or give;
Ends so polarized and ready to live;
Charging into realms;

Electrically charged;
Pulsating to stay alive;
So afraid of touching; always wanting to survive;

So afraid of exploding;
And never ready to die
They assumed the other side was doomed;

So they didn't even try
To go beyond
Their sum zero game;

For the old boys
Were always told
Never to cry.

Must stay brave
While they decorate
Their cave

While they insinuated
They felt their hatred grow
Into tomorrow

Hardened them from their sorrow.

II
Old Boys
Push us aside

EPICS 4

To protect their pride

So close to the end of life
They disempower others
For confidence sake

While they are withering away
We thank the dimensions of power
Overhead and in between

And the power we have never seen
Brings to our ears
The noise of the sea

And the courage to stay free.

III
Sell out
Shake out
Push those with no power out

Act of aggression
Manipulate
Through suggestion

We forget
All blood is red;
We fight for the right

For the power of the day
To rule
In the cruelest way;

Part of the game;
To never remember a name
Unless to blame.

Hypnotize
Criticize
Scrutinize

Euthanize
Charity
But never equality

Call it 'giving back'
But only day old crumbs
Keep their derivatives for their chums;

Another source;
Sometimes to conspire;
Soon to tire;

EPICS 4

The shower of fire;
The power was taken
Marginalized into a mistaken

Identity
Reduced to tears;
Controlled by fears

Power of Panic
To crash
While we are pulled by the noise of the sea.

No longer able
To hold up
Against vanity's rage;

Tyranny;
Society values
Without warranty;

Blues were felt
While unjust dues
Were paid

To those with good intentions
But could not bend
Or question

The vibes they were about to send;
Without speaking;
The old boys' bones were creaking

While they were shrieking

Marginalizing
And disempowering
The entire Shadow Nation

We were pulled by the noise of the sea;

While others were pulled back into the cave;
The walls were painted as black as black could be;
No light was to shine; made it hard to see;

While the old boys lived in their palace
We in the Shadow Nation
Could not feel malice

For malice was above our status.

V

Quality of consciousness
Internal dimension;
Left alone in the building

That was falling;
No longer building;
Just remembering the fallen;

As we spread ashes near meadows still green
We remember what we try to remember
As the seasons come and go

From January to December.

VI
The lie weaved a web
Deceiving many while they wept;
Evil awoke while others slept.

THE END

S.E. McKENZIE

A COG IN THE MACHINE

#51 A COG IN THE MACHINE
I

We are just a cog in the mean Machine;
Driven by our oneness
And powers that cannot be seen.

Conditioned to thrive
We are ruled by the mean Machine's drive;
The Machine needs us to stay alive;

United we are clear sighted

Never to disconnect
We stand erect and tall
Alone we feel so small.

Disconnected

The mean Machine would be broken
For Unity energizes our dream
Creates feelings of self-worth and value; must be true.

Social Bureaucratic and all powerful
The mean Machine when disconnected
Can make you and unseen powers scream;

I am who I am
Not just part of the mean Machine;
Without you I cannot be true

Or be free enough to be just me;

II

You try to live your dream
But all you hear
Is the mean Machine's scream.

You try;
You cry;
You hear it lie

Every day
Until the day
You die;

You look up into the sky
To see the once living have now gone by,
Without even saying goodbye;

III

He asked for calm
During the storm
All alone and hungry

So many could not get warm.

He knew what I knew
And you knew too
The mean Machine could never cry

And the mean Machine would never die;
The mean machine would always thrive
As long as it had all of us to drive

And keep it alive.

Technology gets complicated
But what is produced
Is over rated

While we the cogs
Feel out dated
And our value is never stated.

Technology increases the underfed's overkill
Decreases the need for goodwill
Between unseen powers;

Behind the mean Machine
Economic input
Output

Chance to get ahead;
Or starve;
Left for dead;

Pity those left out before the final shout;
The ones who are left out sit on the curb;
Some say they want to disturb;

Nowhere else to go
The mean machine attacks their self-worth;
Leaving their mind troubled in self-doubt

With forgotten words they are not allowed to shout.

THE END

FINAL SOLUTION

#52 FINAL SOLUTION
I

Back breaking work
Dulled his mind;
Over time; he grew unkind;

Pessimistic; low expectations of peers;
So controlled by his fears
Did not treat others like brothers;

So pessimistic about the world
And those that shared his ground;
He forgot that true life was round.

He grew killer eyes; always wore a disguise;
Only free to be himself when wearing a mask
He does not speak when you ask

Anything at all;
He would rather push you into the abyss
And see you crawl;

Make you feel small
While climbing his wall;
Never treating others as brothers;

EPICS 4

For him positive thinking
Only happens
When one is drinking.

His toxic word makes others feel absurd;
Professional pessimist;
He spreads dread across the land.

II
My True Love was under his command;
For the Bully Master
Was My True Love's Boss;

Bully Master was always cross.
As the years went by
The stress it grew contributed to my loss;

As my True Love's heart
Broke in two;
I felt all that pain as it grew.

III
Doctor Joe Inc.
Told my True Love to prepare
For death was knocking at our door.

Hand in hand we ran;
Took a plane
And flew away.

Leaving our troubles behind
We saw great beauty
It was our duty

For we were preparing for the end.

IV

Currency falling;
Privacy stalling;
The dispossessed crawling

In the Abyss
Of the new world order
Of Toxic Man;

As hard as steel; Bully Boss
His objectification conditioned him
Not to feel as he demeaned

With his dull wit;
Low expectations
Never treating others like brothers.

V

Systematically; many
Fell into the Abyss
And were never missed.

Thought control; engineered content
Without our consent
Many were poisoned with fear

Whenever someone different
Came near.
Cops wearing riot gear

Feeling under threat;
While me and my True Love
Were not ready to die yet.

We heard death knocking at our door
But we were flying to a land
We had never seen before.

Hand in hand
We heard the trumpets blare
But me and my True Love didn't care;

We were flying above
This land we love
While death machines roamed below.

Bully Master was armed to the teeth
Underneath
Our plane there was so much pain.

Not what we had voted for;
We wanted life
Not war.

But the hooded grim reaper
Was knocking at our door.
Carrying an ax; was there to collect Death Tax.

But me and my True Love
Had flown away
Hand in hand

We could not stay
Another day in that toxic land;
While death was knocking at our door

We were heading to a land
We had never seen before
We could see the giant wall below;

The higher it grew
Fear did too;
But we were flying above every cloud

We were now in a space
Where a few were allowed
To be; yes we were almost free.

VI

Culture manufacturing consent
Of hate
Justification to discriminate

Culture pre-packaged in porn
De-engineered and worn
Unlinked from progress; in a state of distress;

S.E. McKENZIE

The Empress was in a state of undress;
Bully Master was wearing a frown
For someone had stolen his crown

And would not confess.

Bully Master was losing control
The force of Nature was changing his role.
Born to be a poor son he had never known fun.

Living in a beautiful location
They were all fighting
To own the sensation

Living in Paradise lost
The cost
Changed every day;

Price increases never go away
So many people wish they could stay
Once they found Paradise Lost.

EPICS 4

The frown of the Clown
Brought them down
But me and my True Love

Had flown away
To discover what we had missed
While watching so many

Crawling in the abyss;
Dysfunction
Bully Master tried to hide

Dysfunction
Hurts his pride
Dysfunction

Makes him choose a side.
His pessimism takes over;
Watch it spread dread

Across the land
As me and my True Love
Fly overhead

Hand in hand.

Grumpy old men congregate in the cave;
Some cover their age with black hair dye
Others; still not brothers, have hair of straw

And do not try;
So content manufacturing consent
While rewriting the law;

No due diligence needed
As they flex their might;
No concern for another's person's right

While me and my True Love
Were flying
Into the Light.

Bully Master was staring and glaring at you
In the middle of the night;
But me and my True Love

Were holding each other tight.

While the Bully Master
Agreed with the Grim Reaper
That it was

To engineer a climate of fear;
Kept so many
In a state of fight and flight;

More to share
When less people
Are there.

THE END

S.E. McKENZIE

BAIT

#53 BAIT
I
To defy the odds;
To do the impossible
Just to make it possible.

You hear the whistle call
To climb the wall;
That wall that blocked

The unknown to progress;
Uncertainty was the bait
For the nouveau prison state.

The wall
To block outsiders;
The wall

To empower insiders;
The wall
We had to climb

To save Reason
From being tried
For treason.

The ice caps melted away;
The seasons could not stay;
As the earth's axis tilted

Towards my land;
You held my hand
Without any demand

We grew strong
In a new world
Where risk and uncertainty

Felt so wrong;
Fear of the unknown
Weakened the strong.

The fear of the unknown
Made Toxic Man
Take control.

Without a smile
He screamed
Without a smile

EPICS 4

His touch
Was harsh
And callous;

Toxic Man
Fed Malice
Which imprisoned

Hope
Under false pretense.
Without Hope

Love made no sense;
While Toxic Man
Glared and stared

For he had lost his magnetism
A long time ago
Now all he wanted was control.

The sky began to change
And many wondered why;
As the ice caps melted away

While Willful Blindness
Could not see
The new; so stuck

In a time gone by
When the Polar Regions
Had much more ice.

II

The Earth's axis began to sway.
Old measurements
Which were so precise

Were no longer that way.

Old measurements
Were no longer exact
For the tilting axis

Changed that fact.

New shipping routes
Changed the power structure too
Throwing out old world order

For the new;

What was living
To feed the living
Was wilting away;

For the order of the seasons
Could not stay the same way;
For the changing sky

Made it that way.

So that we could be free
From all this fear
Systematic demons

Exploited to regress
What had been
And what could have been

If only the vision had been seen
In the cool morning light
Ghetto-speak made them fight.

III
Predator
Fed on the fish
That fed on the worm

Predator
Owned the sky
Never letting his prey get by.

To defy those things which intimidate;
And to make those things that should be,
Be; so that we can see

The goodness all around; grow
Into tomorrow;
Beyond the wall

That kept the changing world
Out of sight;
Ghetto speak made them fight;

Ignorance stayed below
In the cave;
Ignorance was not that brave;

Could not fly into the sky above
The pulsating sound
Left on the ground

Attracts his prey
In a world
That has lost its way.

IV

Noise screeches;
Harmony teaches;
Vibrations make waves;

Rhythmic
Skin drum
Sets the pace

For the race
Deciding who will win
Who will lose

The Sum Zero game;
On the food chain;
Life and pain;

Creates hysteria;
Watch the Bully Master
Throw a micro portion

Of his money in the air;
Peasants run with hands waving
Fight each other; a break from slaving

And that is all;
Who will climb the wall?
Who will remain on the ground and crawl?

We lost our seasons
As the axis tilted
The flowers wilted

As the ice caps melted
New routes for shipping were devised
Were advised.

Before the ice could melt;
We were so cold;
We were well preserved

We were told.

Hysteria when focused on everything
That does not relate
Mesmerizes

For not just gold
Glitters
When lost in the cold.

V

Iron age
Of Rage
Felt the pull

Felt the push
Some had so much
They always looked full

They cup ran over
And slammed against the wall;
That wall.

The wall we were hiding behind;
Clinging to hop
Just cope.

VI

Even Chaos was lost in this noise;
I heard a voice so faint
In my ear tell me not to fear;

The mask has been lifted
The axis has been shifted
From the center of the Universe

The spin
Led to lost seasons
No reasons

The flood
Turned fresh water
Into mud

While drinking the hero's blood.

THE END

GHOST

#54 GHOST
I

There was a land
Hidden in
Machiavelli Valley

Where rulers ruled
With an iron fist;
Everyone was put on a list.

So polarized
The axis
Was tilting;

And love could not grow
In all the fear
That was near, life was wilting.

Cold air was pumped in; everywhere
It was so cold;
Made us shiver and feel old.

We were all trapped in this land
Hidden in
Machiavelli Valley.

EPICS 4

Disconnected
Alienated
Doctrinated to be strangers;

We were left to fight for crumbs
And overcome dangers;
While the peasant king

Felt so righteous, just a silly little man
Taking whatever he can;
Pushed away those he demanded loyalty from;

Now;
Music that spoke of love was canned;
Mail sent everyday was spammed.

And how they fought
Each other
For the little they got.

They were all pitted
Against each other
While the walls hid the rot.

Judges sent many away
To live in cells
And to work for free all day;

The righteous few threw crumbs to them
Through a slot in the door;
While love was buried somewhere below the floor,

Love remained true.

While the wall hid decay they knew no other way.
The ruler; was just a silly little man;
Ruling with an iron fist the best that he can;

Everyone was put on a list.
Heads bowed down;
Covered with a frown.

II
Once living behind a veil;
She was adorned by ornaments
From head to toe, felt like hell.

The veil hid her face;
The veil hid her beauty;
She was raised to do her duty.

III

She is now a Sad Ghost;
Spirit in the night
Taking flight

Out of sight.
Living in her host
She felt his might;

And he felt no pity;
For love was pure;
Electrifying energy;

Came from the heart;
Pulsating
All night.

Because she was dead
Nothing could be said;
For she was just a Spirit without mass.

She still knew the secret
That grew
And could not pass away.

The secret was here to stay;
Despite what they had to say;
It didn't matter,

It was just that way.

IV
At first no one could see
What such a life
Would grow to be.

Lost people without names,
Buried below our moving feet;
They move so we don't feel defeat.

After the storm the form
Felt no fear,
For Love was near.

As new life grew
It glowed in you
And what was true

Could not be said
For Ghost was dead.
Ghost clung onto her host's heart;

So she could feel it pound;
She preferred this
Than sleeping all alone in the ground;

Always knowing that life was round.

For all Ghost had to hold on to
Was love so true;
Magic that was never gone;

Sang in tune
To his skin drum
Pounding strong and hard.

And Ghost would not let go

From the only world
That she would ever know.
She refused to stay forgotten

While sleeping
In the ground,
So she floated around;

Around the sun;
She yearned
She learned

Not to burn
As she walked
Between the flames

Scorching the earth;
For new life
Was about to begin.

V

At times
We did not have
Enough to eat

EPICS 4

Though we knew
We would always meet
Again in a world without pain.

We could only see the heavens
In the night's sky;
For the morning sun

Brought too much light
Though the warmth gave us might
To stand upon our feet

Though we did not have enough to eat
We knew we would always meet
Again.

Upon this space below;
There was too much fear
For love to grow.

We felt the wind coming
From all directions
And we hid in the cave;

Not because we were not brave;
But it was time for us
To fall into a deep sleep.

VI

Ghost stayed awake
As she clung to her host's heart
She clung with all her might.

As he ran from the very place
Where she had died;
The place where so many had lied.

Ghost tried
To not be forgotten
And to live forever in memory.

No one knew the truth
Anymore.
We all knew

The story of her lost youth;
She clung to her host's heart
Just to feel the light

EPICS 4

Illuminate
Free from hate
That sealed her fate.

To see the light;
We look up above
And see the face of space

In the night sky.
For Ghost could not leave
The land where she fell.

Without her host's help.
So he carried her away from hell.
They both lived above the ground

And below
The clouds.
Life grew, decayed and died.

The truth of this rhythm
Could not be denied.
Ghost felt objection

But no one knew;
For they could not see her projection
And though her love was true

No one knew

Her lost attributes
Of creativity
For this was the age of destruction

And only a few
Knew
Ghost's gratitude.

As the axis was gaining tilt
Much was about to wilt.
While Ghost's love

Would be forever superior;
Ghost would no longer be treated
As the inferior.

Ghost had no reason
Accept to live in the moment
To enjoy each season

EPICS 4

Ghost's joy could not be spoken;
When her host's power
Had awoken

For Ghost's love could not sleep
Yearned for immortality
And would not weep;

For Ghost clung
To her host's heart
And refused to let go;

While he carried her away
Inside of him
She would stay

And live as the day
Became tomorrow;
She hid from the shadows of sorrow;

For her love would live forever.
Bridging gaps
The way it was meant to be;

While the willfully blind
Refused to see;
The truth was meant to be

Not yet ready to set us free.

For the truth could not be said
For Ghost was dead
And her head

Was buried deep below
Where the living seldom go
Unless they mine

Gold
And other precious metals
Until they grow old.

Unlike Ghost.
Ghost was hidden behind the wall
So no one heard her cry;

No one believed
Such righteous souls
Would lie.

Even when they watched her die.
We all knew,
Only love would act true.

Then we were told that she looked too bold,

So there was no room for her in the sky;
And that is why
Ghost clung onto her host

As they ran from there
Hoping to find someone kind
Beyond Machiavelli Valley.

VII

Ghost could not be seen
For she was living inside her dream
And her host could not leave her behind

Though her buried bones
Were deep in the ground
Never to be found

Ghost's force was turning
Still burning
Still yearning

Still learning
To make the world
A better place.

Then I heard Ghost say;

"We need to make it better today.
For today never ends;
And tomorrow takes too long to come.

For all we have is now.
To make things right."
She said before she floated away

Into the midnight light.

THE END

CHIEF

#55 CHIEF
I

Chief of Machiavelli valley on call,
In charge of relief behind his wall.
His actions are based on his belief

That higher power over others
Is his to snare;
Never to share. never to care;

Blowing cold air everywhere.

Chief makes others feel cold and small
While he takes it all;
Oppressor loves to see others crawl

Higher power over others
Who would never be considered brothers;
In Machiavelli valley.

He is the chief; oblivious to all the grief
He causes when he says you are fired
Now go away, he loves the power to demean.

Caused when he yells and screams
While intruding on sleepers' dreams.
His cold air is everywhere.

Chief says he really does care
For the social welfare of all;
As he demands a higher wall.

Now there is no turning
Until you get to the top of the hill;
The place where they teach you

How to kill for a thrill;
On payday you can pay your bill
In Machiavelli valley.

II
The sun shines
Through the clouds
Only at variable times;

As Chief spreads his cold air everywhere.
He looks at you
As if you are not there;

His angry tone
Controls fate
Contributes to his estate.

Chief blames others
He would never call brothers;
For make believe crimes;

Such trouble gives him authority

To shoot on command;
Does not have to relate;
No empathy building to date;

For the road with no turn
Channels the flow
To the new city; so afraid it may burn.

We all hold on
To see the morning light;
Even though we are picked on;

By the elite who are paid to fight
And process
The regression creating a new recession,

EPICS 4

Up on the hill;
The place where pretty faces
Greet you and shake your hand

Before they kill you
On command
In Machiavelli Valley.

Absolute power is Chief's only hope
To cope
As he ages; he rages

Blowing his cold air everywhere

Even at those sitting in the sun
Peeking out through the cloud
At variable times.

As chief gets his power
When he accuses others
Never called brothers, of make believe crimes;

As his power grows;
His wealth shows;
On display, for all to see;

S.E. McKENZIE

From his tower
Of power
Sits a flower

Reminds him of the lady with the rose
Who arose; she knows;
As she grows

Still frozen in time
While chief
Blows cold air everywhere.

Chief would have it all while others had none.
Chief is a sad man
Lets his anger grow out of control,

To abuse, to use, to misuse;
A way of life; to oppress for fun;
While there is no turning you must run

Until you have found
The new city
Which breeds and feeds from war.

EPICS 4

There you will be greeted
By a pretty face
Who would just love to splatter

Your blood all over the place.

Hate grows and needs relief
And the chief
Grows oblivious to the grief;

Deceit hid what was yet to come
On the road of no turning
Just burning without learning;

Repeating history;
Power just for the few,
Leaving the rest in misery.

Optimism for a fool;
Pessimism works for those that rule;
Spilling blood makes them drool;

Up on the hill
Where they learn to kill
For a thrill.

On payday
You get to pay your bill
In Machiavelli Valley

Where they have no promises to keep;
They might kill you in your sleep;
Leaving your loved ones all alone to weep.

III

Chief's power is fixed in a charade;
He is the happiest when he is on parade.
He yells and screams

Just to destroy her dreams;
For her happiness
Makes him envious;

His anger grows
Toxic and venomous;
He creates problems out of nothing at all

So that he has an excuse
To build a wall;
An excuse to ghettoize

Others until they feel so small.

Culture of anger empowers his schemes;
He puts out the pressure
And destroys her dreams.

"More for me," he says in glee;
He counts his gold
And pile of cash

While he hides it all in his stash
In a drawer, on his side of the wall;
Leaving others with nothing at all.

He sits on his throne
Reading magazines
Pictures of girls he will never know

While he grows treasure;
For his pleasure;
Value that he can measure.

IV

Chief blames the aggregate;
He wants to segregate
The haves from the have nots.

He doesn't know how things work;
He yells and screams and acts like a jerk;
For his culture of anger seems to work.

He blames the woman with the rose
He grows problems
From nothing real at all

So he can build his wall.
He accuses; he abuses;
He never allows her in, or to begin.

V

Chief speaks of revolution
And the final solution;
While he keeps the air cold

And unpleasant;
His tyranny
Is forever present;

While super bombs
Are detonated
He wonders why he is so hated.

EPICS 4

Even though he says that love is over rated.
He wishes that he could be part of the scene
He sees in his magazine.

He lives in a mansion
And has a few more;
He has objects of luxury

Piled from ceiling to floor
While locking out his creditor
Standing behind his armored door.

For his creditor is demanding more.
Chief knows what he owes
But can still get more

The way he has done
Many times before.
While others have hardly anything at all

He lives his life of luxury
Behind his wall.
Air he pumps out is too cold and too hot

You say anything you might get shot.

And near-slaves work
Just to eat
While he yells out

"Accept defeat."
Nothing will grow
In the place we will force you to go.

Culture of anger dominates;
As he stomps his boots, he agitates;
Nothing matches his expensive suits; he aggregates.

Within his culture of anger; he delegates
The lady with the rose; who arose as she grows.
Chief never lets her in;

So she has nowhere to begin.
Many say Chief is a jerk,
But they tremble when he is near,

His manufactures anger
So he can rule by fear.
He wasn't too smart

EPICS 4

When he closed his heart;
Now he is willing to tear others apart.
He manufactures conflict

Out of nothing at all
So he can build
His multi-billion dollar wall.

Hear him scream;
See him destroy the dream
His face is distorted when he looks so mean.

During this time that many try to economize
He attacks them with stereotypical lies,
Waiting to hear their cries

As the dream wilts away and dies.
His generals eat well
While they plan a living hell;

As he builds his wall
Between the haves and have nots;
Things that can't grow; will decay then rot.

Chief does not know how things work;
He gets by because he acts like a jerk;
He never lets her in; nowhere for her to begin;

No entry point;
"And why should there be,"
He yells and shouts out;

"There will be more just for me."

Legislated poverty
Contributes to his wealth
While he brags about his health.

He fears those who have forbidden knowledge;
The tool for those who refuse
To be treated like a fool.

Forbidden knowledge;
The power of vision and sight;
Gained while reading all night

In artificial light.

EPICS 4

Chief's belief leads to grief;

While the lady holding on to the rose
Holds on with all her might
She waits for the morning light;

The lady with the rose arose and grows.

So strong, Chief won't let her in
She has nowhere to begin.
And all he can see is her skin.

THE END

SCORNed

#56 SCORNed
I

Born into a world that was torn
By Slander and Division,
Fragile Ego; opposing position;

Could never make a good decision
Their scope of vision
Was so narrow it caused sorrow;

Many were caught up in the moment
And forgot
About Tomorrow.

Making each other's lives as hard as can be;
So willfully blind, they could not see;
The Malice was started

In the very cold hearted as they manipulate;
Emotionally charged into the Negative State;
How they loved the power of their growing Slander and Hate.

Without Equity; turned others into the Enemy;
Creating Negative Chemistry;
Emotionally charged; almost in Ecstasy;

Negative Bias
Fed a polarized world of Slander and Division;
Self-fulfilling prophecy; manufactured this condition.

In a roundabout way every day;
They fed Negative Bias so it never went away;
Fools believed everything Bias had to say;

For Negative Bias
Came before the Fall;
For it made fools out of nothing true at all.

Kept Life's disappointments at bay;
Fed Negative Bias
And defamed every day.

Hoping that those they hated
With all their Heart, would soon be part
Of the Departed.

To escape scorn, we were too willing to be torn;
Never needing to be warned;
Under the design of the Glass Ceiling.

EPICS 4

We knew Negative Bias was always feeding;
And we would die too soon;
But for Negative Bias, it was never soon enough.

Our Enemy gave us a ladder to climb;
So that we could reach higher in Time;
If Time were only on our side.

Even though the Glass Ceiling cuts our flesh.
Our Free Spirit moves us along
Invisible to Negative Bias so near us and so wrong.

While many volunteered to be deleted
We refused to be defeated'
We exist with a right to be, you and me,

Which could transcend
Beyond expectations.
Visible in mass

Brick by brick
The wall grew to be
Less transparent; made Context harder to see;

Scope of Vision
So narrow
They could never be free;

So they allowed Negative Bias
To control
Their Destiny.

Worshipped by the Heir Apparent;
Rigid, frigid, no positive feeling;
Only way out was through the Glass Ceiling;

Negative Bias;
It stared, it glared, it shared;
Was always ready for feeding;

While you were smashing through the Glass Ceiling;
You were hurting but ignored all feeling;
Slander and Division; futile to resist

For only a few would ever be missed;
Most were trapped in the feeding
Of the Negative Bias so near us.

EPICS 4

The Power Clique owned it all;
Loved to make others crawl
And feel small before the Fall.

You must play their game and that is all.
Don't let them know how you feel;
For they will kick you down again;

Why should they care?
After they destroy their targets,
They are out of there.

The Enemy gives purpose
And a ladder to climb;
Now you can say "I am who I am."

As you smash through the Glass Ceiling
Negative Bias
Always needs feeding.

For you to escape all the Unfair Dealing
You must climb and avoid distraction.
While they get so much satisfaction

When they say with nose in the air
"We will make your life really hard,
For we own it all and we don't care,

We can make you crawl
For we owe you nothing at all."
They warned; they scorned;

While Goodwill's heart was broken in two;
There was not much
Anyone could do;

For it was all rigged in Negative Bias.

"As you get upset;
We will hang up the phone;
Leave you all alone;

For you know;
There is one way out,"
They said with scorn;

But they were wrong; we were strong;

Only way out was through the Glass Ceiling;
We would be cut and torn;
We were too aware that we didn't care;

EPICS 4

Even though life is round for ever more
We arose from the ground
To be devastated no more;

And what was manipulated
Will pass in Machiavelli Valley,
While some of it remains

In ruins; still, there are gains;
Temporary life
Comes before Death

Existence without breath.
That day we dread;
Gone; we are dead.

To lie so still
Against one's will
After living life's power

In motion
Moving
So alive on a planet

We never chose;
But lived on; never as one;
Always to be opposed by opposition

Slander and Division;
Toxic for the human condition
Lying in the Superior Position.

The miracle of it all.
The wonder is forgotten
When hunger pangs strike.

Man's cruelty to man
Invisible, ignores content;
Assumes intent;

Manufactured consent
To keep divided
What should have been whole.

The love of gold before the Fall
Brought us doom;
Such love pulled us into opposing directions.

EPICS 4

At times we could not choose our selections.
The moment would pass
Forgotten, it could never last.

For we were so slight
Pitted against the might
Which was always out of sight;

The Mysterious Force
Behind it all could never be seen;
Some wondered if it had ever been

More than just a dream.

How could such turmoil been overseen;
Suffering that we never chose
We were knocked down to the ground

Then we arose.

We were born;
Into a world so torn;
So much was already worn.

Our pangs of hunger
Controlled who we could be
What we could see

The beauty around us.
The world we know
Had a mysterious source

In time
So long ago
How were we to know?

II

Energy that thrives
Keeps us alive
Gives us drive; to stay

And struggle for another day.

Even though they like to say so
They fill your mind with worry
Slander and division;

EPICS 4

Unmanaged uncertainty
Makes it hard
To make a decision.

They are always in a hurry;
They own what you never will;
No stakeholder theory here;

Just fear; on the road with no turn;
Living in a city
Just waiting to burn.

III

Dark bands
Invisible Hands
Such a Force understands

We hope to see
The sea rush in
When high tide is due,

I will be waiting for you.

We look through clouds
Until the atmosphere
Reaches space hoping to see a face

Of a life restored,
Somehow if it could be
Brought back to Earth.

But the Force we could not see
Would not let such a thing be;
Their return was forbidden.

For their time, like grains of sand

Had been spent
And controlled by the Invisible Hand.
So their life could never be lived again;

They would never return here
The place where they created so much fear
With their Slander and Division;

Beneath the atmosphere
Covering the ground
We could hear the harmony in all the sound.

EPICS 4

Rules by their love of gold, their cold heart
Could still pound
And we wondered how.

The land was no longer ours;
Owned by the bank;
And hidden by walls;

We felt the connection anyway
For without the land
We would have nowhere to stand.

We hid behind the trees;
We saw our reflection
In the lake;

There was no mistake;
We were alive; we had survived;
So we were still able to be

Until we were alive no longer.

Starvation on this side of the wall
Was common
Though not seen at all.

Paradise was everywhere and was not lost;
Just out of reach;
Never ours;

Owned by the bank
That kept paper bills
Which had written:

"In God We Trust"
All over them,
Near the ever-seeing eye.

The lie grew
Until many
Thought it must be true.

The walls hid what would be self-evident
If only could be seen;
Walls hid what once was;

For walls could never be transparent;
And walls were worshipped
By the Heir Apparent.

IV

We found a place still not ours
We stared at the moon for many hours
We slept amongst the flowers.

We knew we would die too soon;
For we lacked the paper which broke bias
For a moment, the ever-seeing eye would still deny us;

Disconnected from the Order
We could not die
Soon enough for them

While they bathed in Slander and Division
Allowed them to cloud
Their vision.

For the men of gold
Did not cherish love
For they were too cold.

While the land was left to grow back to nature
Until it was bought.
We knew if we were found there

We could be shot.
Wars between the haves and have nots
Continued to be true through history of misery.

The order, closed doors
To reason for others
Saved it for their chosen brothers.

Such decay in no man's land
Brought new life onto the Earth
But could never return the old.

From generation to generation
That is all we knew
And all we could see to be true

For the air around us
Was still transparent
And was there to share.

Death could not smile
It was just there
And we journeyed to it;

EPICS 4

Every one of us
Would soon see the other side;
Maybe we would find mercy there;

For the world as we knew it was hostile to the poor;
And the bank changed locks on so many doors
We couldn't care anymore.

For we found our cave,
And returned to it
The way life might one day be

With purpose just to see.

V

Our feet march to war
Crushing flowers
Like many times before.

There was no harmony
And how could there be
For the Negative Bias controlled Destiny.

Our heavy hearts pound
Until some are shot to the ground
Never to hear another sound.

We wait for a signal from the State
To end this madness
But it came too late.

Cities were designed to channel traffic one way;
Created wealth for some
In the usual way;

Slander and Division
Disconnected the Innocent
From the Final Decision with Suspicion.

They hated; they grated until the Nerves had awoken;
They could not scream out, they were too broken.
The Power Clique would use everything said

Against them; for Negative Bias was in control of their head;
We knew we would die too soon
For them it would never be soon enough.

EPICS 4

Rigid was death in a world with too little love.
Paradise was paved
While the defamers said they would have saved

All those who confessed
To Slander and Division
Knew it was a terrible decision

To live under such Suspicion;

For Negative Bias
Had surrounded us
In this madness and Hell.

In their order it shaped every role;
And those without the paper
Of the ever-seeing-eye, would face Negative Bias

Alone; just another excuse to deny us;
While they gave us no privacy
In their conspiracy

Of Slander and Division.

Many died too soon under Suspicion,
But not soon enough,
For those who did not care,

But wanted to own everywhere.
They demeaned with their angry tone
To scare those who were all alone;

For in this order;
Power would only flow
In one direction;

In Machiavelli Valley.

For the Enemy gave purpose
And a ladder
To climb.

While the mega walls stopped
Any kind of turning
On the narrow road;

Persecution
By Watchers
Was understood but not revealed.

The divide between religion and science;
New and old;
Love of the Divine Right

And the pursuit of gold all night,

Led to much of the Earth being sold
To the highest bidder;
For the price of a dream and gold.

And we could hear their screams;
As they were reaching for their dreams;
Smashing through the Glass Ceiling;

Was the only way out.

THE END

The Orange Man

#57 THE ORANGE MAN
I

We were warned not to be rude;
We were told not to be crude;
We were ordered about

And demoralized

In a military fashion,
Overheard above forbidden passion,
In a world that needed more love

We all gazed into Heaven above
Not knowing
Where to turn.

We heard Nouveau Gestapo
Shout Out
An order or two

We had no idea
What he was about to do.
As he yelled over Co-motion, he said,

"Life is not art
It is okay
To tear it all apart."

We were warned not to be rude
We were told not to be crude
By the prude

II

As she reached for the pie in the sky
A warhead flew by;
And she said life is not art

And soon that warhead will tear it all apart."

And that warhead said in defiance,
"Life is not an exact science
All I want to do is hold you tight

Late at night

But I know I would kill you
With all my might,
For I am just a tool for a fool

Never wanting to be so cruel;
Not knowing which way to turn
When another place is about to burn."

And we could see
And tried not to be
Demoralized by the prude

Who calls us rude and crude
Behind her sneer,
We try not to get lost in all her fear.

And the warhead said,
"I fly in the sky
At the speed of light

I am told that life is not art
Still I do not want to tear it apart
Because without life where do we start?

I was just made to give
The other side of the border a fright
New order from the Orange Man

But all I want to do is live
And make love all night
Without crushing everyone in sight.

Even though you know where it will all end
How do you grow
When you can't bend?"

And then I saw the Orange Man
Kneel to what he thought was Glory
He wanted to live the story

He wrote in a note on his boat.

Even though he would be booed
By the prude
For he was sounding so rude

Now he was screwed
For he really was crude
And he needed a change in attitude.

He was just the Orange Man
Waving the flag for all to see
Where he really wanted to be.

III

Then we heard the warhead sing a song
He said we should love one another
And sing along

For killing would always be wrong.

And the prude told us not to be rude
One more time again
For she had pushed us through

The revolving door
Like she had done
Many times before

While the Orange Man
Had a plan to grow stronger
He would divide and conquer

All we felt was repression and anger
For the prude had drained us of our energy
Our life force, our will to stay free.

That was all that we wanted to be.

Then we heard the warhead cry out
In the middle of the night
Vowing to the world that it would not fight.

But the Orange Man
Had another plan
To get even

For what?
Very few knew;
But for now

The black sky was turning blue.

THE END

DEATH
SHADOW

#58 DEATH SHADOW:
End Of The World
I

Death shadow
Was out of sight
Though we could all feel

Its growing might

Following you and me
Whenever there was light
Shining from the blue sky.

Now under suspicion
We weren't allowed
To make a decision

In our own interest
We had to do without
Couldn't scream, couldn't shout.

The world
Was now crueler
We had a new ruler.

As he grew more wealthy
We felt less healthy
And looked into the sky for Hope.

EPICS 4

Love was not enough
Anymore;
We heard the closing of every door

Just like before every war.

And the rain came down in torrents
And soaked into the ground
It was the end of our world

Though Life remained round.

And as the sky turned black
Before our life was gone
We begged for it all back.

Impersonal and difficult;
Robot-thoughts fed
The Shallow-minded hiding behind

Death Shadow;
The way it would be
As they pushed us into Eternity

Before our time.

What should have been
Was never seen
So we were left moving against the wind.

II

As Terror King's temper
Added to the storm
We were pushed away and never warned;

Still looking for a place to stay warm;
Terror King raged and flamed
He pointed fingers at everyone he blamed.

Shallow thinkers
Hiding behind
His Death Shadow

Took over his mind
How could he ever be kind
Death Shadow left him willfully blind.

III

Pushed from here
We refused to be filled with Fear
For we knew there was a stronger power

EPICS 4

Than Terror King's
Fierce fiery shower
While he lived in his ivory tower

How he loved to flaunt his power
As he waved to those who bowed to him
Standing on the street under his tower.

Terror King
Destroyed Love
So we looked above

Into Eternity,
The void; black space
Hid Death Shadow's face

Though we could feel the spirit
Of the raging flame
While he named the ones he blamed

For his loss
He felt it was his
Birth right to be the boss.

So far away from the place
We now called home;
Gave us shelter

From the wind
As it blew
So much of what we knew away

All day
And into the night
The wind blew.

IV

Some felt fright
And then alienation's might
While the world was turned upside down

For Terror King gained
As he lied
While we cried.

Below our place in the sky;

EPICS 4

Changing day by day
Just to adapt to the Future
Without Nurture.

The Future so far and out of reach;
Listen to them preach
While they profit from our fall;

Their hands are out
They want it all;
They force us to go away.

Where?
They don't care
They just don't want us here

In this land of Fear.

We are treated like scum
Worse than a bum
But the elite who seem to always eat.

Force us to crawl
Make us feel small
With hands out, they want it all

They turn their heads
They feast.
They get it all.

Before the wind comes
And blows it all away
Nothing is ever able to stay.

As we grow
Into tomorrow
We are followed by Death Shadow;

We all know that one day
Death Shadow
Will come and take our breath away.

And we too
Will be gone
Too soon.

We follow the birds who try
To find the best way to fly
So that we too may find our path

EPICS 4

And a place to call ours
So we can rest
After the aftermath

We hope to find
A place we belong;
So we can recover and grow strong

Without being told we are wrong.

Shadow; a dark area
In between you and me
And a ray of light

In my space
In my face
Time shines

Entangled
Within a dimension
Never seen

Beyond the flatness
Some believe is Earth's Nature
Missing the wholeness and all its worth

Lost Nurture

We start at Zero
As we walk into Tomorrow;
And so does Death Shadow.

We choose a path that was open to us
We avoided those
Who would see us and make a fuss.

We decided which way to try,
We had no time
To stop and cry.

The world would never be the same.
Now we were only numbers
No one asked our name.

Together we were strong
Still, we had nowhere to belong
As Love grew while she sang her song.

THE END

THE
MORNING
AFTER

#59 The Morning After
I

The New King had been appointed
Dreamer's dreams had been exploited
While my True Love lay in my arms

Everything was uncertain that day.
Dreamer felt my pain;
When he awoke

No one spoke.

So he felt my pain again;
Toxic, chaotic,
Hypnotic.

Dreamer was told to bow down to the New King
Who sold Dreamer's dream for gold in the cold rain
New King; highest member of the Master Class,

Always unseen.

II

Dreamer walked in haste
No time to waste
For he was being hunted down

Dreamer was denied access to the town;
No longer affordable; we cried, they lied.
Prices were fixed; marked up, not down.

Forbidden to enter any door
Or hold legal tender any more
Could not buy food at any store.

Beastly Force was unstoppable;

Dreamer prayed for a miracle that was durable;
Anything less
Would make life horrible;

Not tolerable. Undesirable;
One could not say out loud
That the True Nature of the Beast.

Was deplorable;
For we were not allowed
To feel so proud.

In the Wasteland
Of Despair
Dreamer was doomed if he was

I too awoke to a new world
So unfair
I missed my old world that used to be there.

New King felt no remorse when being mean;
So much was happening behind the scene;
The new rule was cruel

By design
He had the sole right to define
What was right

What was wrong
What was weak
What was strong.

And how else could he win
When everything was dying
Before it could begin?

In the Wasteland
Everyone was crying
No time to find out if the N

EPICS 4

No time for verifying.
How the New King laughed
When he refused to say

Who was going to pay
For the hunters
Who would hunt down

Those on the New King's list
Left by the old King
Who would be forever missed;

If Dreamer was found
He would be Hell bound
So Dreamer hid in the morning mist

Never knowing what the plan was going to be
Sun was not showing
Even though it was the dawning of a new day;

A new way, a new game to play
Called Sum zero;
Dreamer would now be playing it all day.

And I, tried not to cry
As my true love was at Heaven's door
I held out my hand

And begged my True Love
To come back to me
So I could see

The divine
In this Wasteland
All around me

I needed to see
I needed to understand
Through my Love's eyes

So pure to be sure;

The only cure for my doubt
That troubled Dreamer's mind
Was my True Love's love that was so kind.

If True Love could only come alive in me
I would grow to see
Something beyond all this insanity.

III
New King's hierarchy fed
From our energy;
Could only grow

From our spilled blood.
New King dragged our names in the mud;
While he bragged that he was a stud.

IV
Some said I held my True Love
Too tight that night
But True Love's arms were around me

While the dream shattered
And Death was at my door
I held on to my True Love

Tighter than I had ever done before.

V
We needed reassurance;
And how they laughed
Cause we were in the way

As the New King
In his tower of power
Blocked Dreamer's way.

Uncontrollable
Deplorable
Was the New Beast's Way.

Dreamer ran away
Could not stay
For Yesterday was no more.

Even though we still believed
In the dream we had yesterday
Our names were on the list

Of who was to be hunted today.
The list
Would never fade away.

That is what we were told
Anyway;
That our names on the list

EPICS 4

Would stay
Unless they were deleted
By a computer error;

Our names would be on New King's list
For ever;
Soon we would be hunted down

And thrown out of town.

Today was the Morning After
And we felt so weak;
We hoped to grow stronger

Before tomorrow;

The day was his to define;
For he was the New King;
He now controlled everything.

While Dreamer's life was no longer his to define
Future was no longer yours or mine;
Time, once held promise, now led to fear.

A world we could never own;
Guards of stone stared at us
When we were all alone;

The Master Class lorded over us
Grew our Vulnerability;
We never thought we could be free again

From the pain all around
That was soaking into the ground
Without a sound

Again, for it was the morning after
And what we had hoped for
Would never happen;

For soon there would be more war.

How the New King loved to play with our minds.
He loved to play with the rules too;
He treated us like fools;

EPICS 4

He lied so much
We never knew
What was true.

Our uncertainty
Made him laugh
In the aftermath

Of what he had done.
We wanted what we had yesterday back;
But our pain came rolling in again

With the rain.

VI

Uncontrollable
It was all a game
The New King liked the role

He was about to play

He chose who to blame
Who to name;
Within the hierarchies

He would build
And tear down;
His smile could quickly turn into a frown.

VII

Master Class power
Was uncontrollable
Some lived in bunkers

That were not noticeable.

Some lived in the Ivory Tower
Of illusion
Caused so much confusion;

Selling us a dream
That could never be;
Now we see the changing of the guard;

Happened before;
Behind the closed door;
Manufacturing consent;

The New King raised the rent;
So the promise
Could be broken

EPICS 4

And our pain
Had awoken
Hypnotic, Chaotic,

Now the nightmare
Would begin
They told us our existence was a sin.

They took our money to burn
At the end of every year
We waited for our turn

But it never came.

THE END

Produced by S.E. McKenzie Productions
First Print Edition November 2016

Enquiries: 1(778)992-2453
Mailing Address:
S. E. McKenzie Productions
168 B 5^(th) St.
Courtenay, BC
V9N 1J4

Email Address:
messidartha@aol.com

http://www.amazon.com/SarahMcKenzie/e/B00H9RWX48/

www.ingramcontent.com/pod-product-compliance
Lightning Source LLC
Chambersburg PA
CBHW061144040426
42445CB00013B/1539